THE

D1767011

Literacy

by
Deborah Crisfield

CRESTWOOD HOUSE

New York

Maxwell Macmillan Canada
Toronto

Maxwell Macmillan International
New York   Oxford   Singapore   Sydney

LIBRARY OF CONGRESS CATALOGING-IN-PUBLICATION DATA

Crisfield, Deborah.
　　The facts about literacy / by Deborah Crisfield. — 1st ed.
　　　p.　　cm. — (Facts about)
　　Includes glossary/index.
　　Summary: Discusses the problem of illiteracy, different ways in which people learn to read, and resources available to those with reading difficulties.
　　ISBN 0-89686-750-1
　　1. Functional literacy—United States—Juvenile literature.　2. Literacy programs—United States—Juvenile literature.　3. Reading—United States—Juvenile literature.　[1. Literacy.　2. Reading.]　I. Title.　II. Series.
LC151.C75　　1992
302.2′244—dc20　　　　　　　　　　　　　　　　　　　　　　91-39567

PHOTO CREDITS

all photos by Richard Bachmann

CRESTWOOD HOUSE

Crestwood House
Macmillan Publishing Company
866 Third Avenue
New York, NY 10022

Maxwell Macmillan Canada, Inc.
1200 Eglinton Avenue East
Suite 200
Don Mills, Ontario M3C 3N1

Macmillan Publishing Company is part of the Maxwell Communication Group of Companies.

First edition
Printed in the United States of America

10　9　8　7　6　5　4　3　2　1

CONTENTS

LEARNING TO READ

Martha studied the word carefully. This one was longer than the words she was used to. She didn't know if she could read it.

"Sound it out," said Elizabeth. "It's not as hard as it looks."

Martha sounded it out slowly, using all the tricks that Elizabeth had taught her. "Mushroom," she said at last. "The word is mushroom."

Elizabeth was very proud of Martha. She was learning to read, and Elizabeth was helping her. Martha wasn't a child. She was 52 years old.

Elizabeth and Martha were working together to develop Martha's reading skills. One of Martha's goals was to be able to read the labels in the grocery store. Before Martha began working with Elizabeth, Martha could only buy food that had pictures on the label.

When Martha's granddaughter asked her to make tomato soup, she didn't know what to do. The soup cans didn't have pictures on them. Which one was tomato? Martha guessed and opened one of them, but it was cream of broccoli. When Martha saw how upset her granddaughter was, she decided it was time to learn to read.

Most people learn to read when they are children. They usually learn the alphabet first. Then, in the first grade, they start putting the letters together to make words. Soon they are reading whole sentences. But

People of all ages can learn to read.

some people don't learn to read until much later. Others never learn at all.

Reading is one of the most important skills a person can have. Despite this fact, most of us take reading for granted. And there is more to reading than being able to read for fun. Books are only a small part of the whole reading picture. Nearly everything we do requires reading.

Visiting someone on the other side of town can be impossible for a person who can't read street signs. A nonreader can't look in the yellow pages for a plumber. Even more importantly, someone who can't read won't be able to understand hospital instructions or the label on a bottle of medicine. Not being able to read can be a very serious problem.

For a nonreader, trying to understand a street sign can be scary and confusing.

LITERACY

The official government definition of *literacy* is "using printed and written information to function in society, to achieve one's goals and to develop one's knowledge and potential." It sounds pretty complicated, but it isn't. Literacy means having the ability to read.

Not being able to read is called *illiteracy*. There are very few people today who are completely illiterate. Most people are able to read their names or the word "Stop" on a stop sign. They might even be able to read an easy book. But if they can't read enough to get by in today's world, they are called *functionally illiterate*. People who are functionally illiterate might not be able to read a newspaper article, a cookbook or a note sent home by a teacher.

TIMES ARE CHANGING

There are very few totally illiterate people in this country, and the numbers are improving. But there are many functionally illiterate people. And because this world is getting more and more complicated, it is harder to survive without being able to read.

Since the 1950s, Ernie has worked for a small furniture company, making chairs. When he began working

7

for the company, all the work was done by hand. Ernie didn't know how to read, but it didn't matter. He didn't need reading skills to build chairs.

Ernie's son Jay started helping his father when he was very young. He was going to make chairs too. It didn't seem important for Jay to go to school. His father could teach him everything he wanted to know.

But when Jay was old enough to go to work, the furniture company made a change. They brought in machines to make the chairs. They still kept a few employees who made chairs the old way, but all the new people had to be able to run the machines. They gave Jay a manual. He couldn't read it, so he wasn't able to run the machines. The company fired Jay.

Jay applied for jobs at other places. It was the same everywhere. Some places even wanted him to know how to use a computer. Jay couldn't hold the same job his father held. He learned that making chairs today requires the ability to read.

LOOKING AT THE NUMBERS

The U.S. Department of Education has done studies on the reading ability of Americans. They have discovered that 20 percent of Americans are functionally illit-

For a nonreader it can be impossible to tell one soup can from another.

erate. Most of these people have trouble doing simple tasks like addressing an envelope.

Another 34 percent aren't literate enough to do well in today's world. These people may be able to write their address, but they can't read a machine's manual, an insurance form or even the help wanted section in the newspaper.

If you add 20 percent and 34 percent together, you can see that over half of the country isn't reading as well as it should.

Life is very difficult if you can't read. You can't get a driver's license. You can't vote. You can't read important documents. You can't even read a menu when you go out to eat.

Not being able to read can also be dangerous. What if a mother can't read the directions on a bottle of medicine she has to give her baby? What if a man taking a walk through a field can't read the warning sign for the electric fence?

For a long time, jobs on farms or in factories were good jobs for illiterate people. They didn't need to learn to read to do their jobs well. But today, these jobs require reading skills. It has become more important than ever for people to learn to read.

WHERE DID IT ALL START?

Reading and writing have been around almost as long as people have been on earth. But in the beginning they were very different from the reading and writing we know today.

The earliest people we know about communicated by talking. They created and used a spoken language. But if they couldn't get their ideas across, they drew pictures. These pictures are called *pictographs*. Pictographs were the start of reading and writing.

Some people didn't draw very well. This was a problem because no one knew what their pictures meant.

Other people wanted to draw ideas instead of single objects. But there were no pictures that expressed these ideas. Something else had to be invented.

First, *symbols* were invented. The Egyptians and the Chinese came up with symbols at about the same time. Symbols were easy marks that everyone could draw. Each symbol had a specific meaning. People even invented symbols that stood for ideas. It was very difficult to remember all the symbols and what they stood for.

Finally, the people of the Middle East created an alphabet. With an alphabet, there are only a certain number of symbols for people to remember. These symbols are called letters. Each letter stands for a different sound. The letters are combined to make words. We still use the alphabet system today.

The alphabet system sounds simple, but it does have some problems. Different languages use different alphabets. And sometimes the rules for the sounds of letters are very confusing. Many letters sound different depending on the words they are used in.

The English language has many inconsistencies. Listen to the "g" sounds for "gem" and "gum." They're different. And sometimes letters are silent, like the "g" in the word "light." Compare "foot" and "boot." Why are these words pronounced differently when they are spelled almost exactly the same?

The English language is full of quirks. This is probably because it came from so many different languages. These quirks make it one of the hardest languages to learn.

PLAYING THE GAME

Because English is confusing, it takes a lot of schooling to learn to read and write it correctly. Everyone in the United States is required to go to school from age 5 to 16. This should be plenty of time to learn to read. Unfortunately, our school system doesn't always work well. In fact, at least 27 million Americans have never really learned to read. Some of these people have even made it to college. How does this happen?

Chuck is a good example. Basketball was the only thing he cared about. He played basketball all day long,

Some schools and coaches place too much emphasis on athletics and not enough on academics.

except when he was forced to be in school. Sometimes he even cut school to play basketball. He was the best player in his neighborhood. He was hoping to make it to the pros.

In ninth grade, Chuck's English teacher almost flunked him. She said he could barely read his own name. Chuck was worried. If he flunked, he would be kicked off the basketball team. He talked to his coach. The coach wanted Chuck to play on the team too. The coach and the teacher worked it out. Chuck agreed to get extra help from a tutor so that his teacher wouldn't flunk him.

Chuck worked with the tutor a little bit, but it was interfering with his basketball. It wasn't long before he gave up on the tutoring. It was easier to cheat off someone else's test.

Every time Chuck was in trouble at school, his coach would help him out. Chuck got a basketball scholarship to a big university. Even at college, there were people to help him get by without reading. Everyone understood that, for Chuck, basketball was the most important thing.

Everything was fine until Chuck ruined both of his knees. He couldn't play basketball anymore. His dream of going to the pros was ruined. He didn't know what to do. He couldn't even read the help wanted ads to find out where the jobs were. Chuck's high school coach hadn't done him any favors when he allowed him to graduate without learning to read.

Chuck's situation is more common than people think. But there are many other reasons why people don't learn to read. A child may often miss school because of illness. Another child may have moved a lot during the school year. Often the schools are to blame. Sometimes it is a parent's fault. There are almost as many different reasons for illiteracy as there are illiterate people.

DROPOUTS

School was boring. When James went, he would slouch down in his chair and hope that the teachers wouldn't notice him. He never answered their questions, and most of the time they just left him alone.

James was 16, and he was still in the eighth grade. It seemed to him that he would be 90 years old before he graduated from high school. He wasn't going to wait that long. He wanted to go to work, so he dropped out.

It seemed like the best thing to do at the time, but not for long. James couldn't get any of the jobs he wanted because he couldn't read. He couldn't even fill out a job application. James finally got a job at an animal shelter, hosing down the floors. It was worse than being at school.

Many Americans drop out of school. The dropout rate in this country is about 27 percent. In Japan, only 5 percent drop out. In Russia, only 2 percent drop out. Dropouts are a big problem in this country.

Strong reading skills help kids get ahead.

In many United States cities, more people drop out than graduate. Dropouts usually don't read well. Because potential dropouts aren't good readers, they can't do the work in any of their classes. School is a struggle, and it seems easier to leave. But once you are a dropout, life becomes more difficult.

MISSING OUT

Isabel is a slightly different case. She wanted to be in school. But when she was seven, she developed leukemia. She was in and out of hospitals all the time. Often she

15

was too sick to work with the tutor. Isabel was cured by the time she was nine, but she'd lost a lot of schooltime.

Isabel went back to school and was placed in the fourth grade. But her classmates had had more reading practice. Isabel could only read a few of the words in her schoolbooks. She tried to figure out what the lessons were about from the few words that she knew. Sometimes she was close enough to fool the teachers. They didn't want to push her because they knew she had been sick. But Isabel got farther and farther behind her classmates, and no one seemed to notice or care.

Despite her problems, Isabel stayed in school. She knew she was smart. She had been a good student before she was sick. She just needed extra help to catch up. But the teachers were busy with all the other students. They didn't have time to help Isabel on a one-to-one basis. They let Isabel get away with a lot because they felt sorry for her. Isabel graduated from high school, but she never learned to read.

A BAD EXPERIENCE

As Isabel's experience shows, the way teachers treat a student can make a difference. There are many different teaching styles. What works for some students might not work for others.

Seven-year-old Doug had a bad experience with the wrong teaching style. In the beginning of second grade,

Doug was excited about learning to read. He'd made some progress the year before, and he thought he could only get better. He was wrong.

Doug's second grade teacher liked to have students take turns reading out loud in front of the whole class. Doug didn't like this. He read slower than everyone else, and he made a lot more mistakes. But the teacher asked Doug to read more than the other students. She said that practice would make him a better reader.

Doug was embarrassed that he was so slow at reading. He became more and more nervous every time the teacher called on him. Instead of improving, Doug's

For a slow reader, reading out loud can be an agonizing experience.

reading got worse. He couldn't even concentrate on the easy words because he was so upset.

It wasn't long before the other kids would complain whenever Doug was chosen to read. They said he read too slowly. They wanted someone else to read. Some kids even made fun of Doug out on the playground.

By the end of second grade, Doug hated reading. He told himself that it was stupid. He decided he didn't need to learn to read, and he stopped trying.

A NEW COUNTRY

Not all reading problems come from a bad experience with school. Some people never even go to school. Silke came to the United States from Germany when she was six years old. She had just started to learn to read in German, but she was taken out of school when she moved. Her father and mother had to work to support the family, so they couldn't take time out to teach Silke. She tried going to school for a while, but she couldn't understand anything her teachers or classmates said. Her parents decided to wait until Silke learned English and then send her to school again.

By the time Silke was eight, she had learned English pretty well. But now she was much older than the other children who were starting school. She was embarrassed about her age. She didn't want to go to school, and her parents didn't force her. Silke was becoming a good seamstress, and she didn't need to learn reading and writing to get a sewing job.

When Silke became an adult, she realized her mistake. She wished that her parents had forced her to go to school when she was younger. She made good money as a seamstress, but she could not get another type of job because she couldn't read.

Silke's experience is common among people who move here from another country. In fact, one-third of the illiterate people in this country don't speak English at home. It's hard for them to go to school where lessons are taught entirely in English. Often they don't go to school at all. They never learn to read or write English, and they also don't learn to read or write their own language because they haven't been in school in their own country.

NONREADERS

Illiteracy among adults is quite common. You might be surprised to learn that the man who paints your house can't read or that the mom next door has trouble reading recipes. There are even nonreaders in college who were accepted by the college or university because of athletic ability.

Many people think of nonreaders as poor people from

Approximately 41 percent of the illiterate people in the United States live in large cities.

the city. This isn't true. In fact, 51 percent of the people who can't read live in small towns or suburbs, 41 percent are from cities and 8 percent are from rural areas.

Other people believe that it is just the black and Hispanic people who are illiterate. This isn't true either. There are almost twice as many illiterate white people (41 percent) as there are illiterate blacks (22 percent) and illiterate Hispanics (22 percent).

However, there are more white people in this country than there are black or Hispanic people. That's the reason why the illiteracy percentage is higher among white people. If you look at the number of illiterate people in each ethnic group, the numbers are highest for nonwhite

20

people. Of all the black people in this country, 44 percent are illiterate. Even worse, 56 percent of Hispanic people are illiterate.

It is true that many illiterate people are poor. Most of the jobs that pay a lot of money require reading skills. If a person can't read, he or she will only be able to get a low-paying job, if any job at all. This is one reason why many illiterate people are poor.

ALL IN THE FAMILY

Often, nonreaders come from families of nonreaders. Parents usually pass on the importance of reading and writing to their children. If they are illiterate, they can't do this. Their children don't get the parental help and support that other children get. It is likely that the children's reading skills will suffer too.

Six-year-old David was having trouble in first grade. He had learned the alphabet in kindergarten. Now it was time to learn to read. Learning to read wasn't easy. He brought home the worksheet his teacher had given him, and he showed it to his mom. She had helped him learn the alphabet, and he wanted her to help him learn to read.

David's mom was illiterate. She couldn't even understand his simple worksheet. But she was too ashamed to tell her son that she couldn't read. She told him that reading was stupid and that he didn't have to bother with the worksheet.

David was confused. His teacher had told him that reading was important. Why did his mom say it wasn't? He didn't know what to do. He just thought that there was no one to help him learn to read.

PARENTS AND KIDS IN SCHOOL TOGETHER

A program in Kentucky is trying to break the non-reader cycle. The program tries to get parents and children to read together. This gives older people who can't

Children whose parents help them with homework are more likely to become good readers.

read the chance to learn how. It also prevents parents from passing on illiteracy to their children.

Parents and preschool children who are involved with the program go to an elementary school three days a week. The parents go to a classroom to learn to read. The children go to another classroom to play.

After a few hours of school, the parents and kids get together again. Sometimes the parents read books to their children. Other times they just play together. Then they all eat lunch together.

After lunch, the parents do volunteer work at the school. The kids take naps. At the end of the day, the parents all get together again. They talk about what it is like to be a parent. They talk about how important it is to get an education.

The program is good for many reasons. First, the parents are learning to read. This will help them feel good about themselves. It will also help them get along better in the world. Second, the parents and children learn that school can be fun. The parents learn that they should encourage their children to do well in school. Finally, the parents feel more comfortable about talking to teachers and getting involved with their children's education.

This program started in Kentucky, but it is spreading all over the country. It can prevent nonreading parents from passing on illiteracy to their children. It also shows young children that school is important. Both parents and children benefit from the Kentucky program.

OTHER PROGRAMS

The Kentucky program is new. It started in 1989. But there are many other literacy programs that have been around for a long time.

One of the first people to start an international organization to teach adults to read was Frank Laubach. He was a minister who taught people to read using the Bible. He became so successful that he needed people to help him teach his students. His program grew and grew. Now it exists in many different countries.

In 1962, a woman named Ruth Colvin decided to fight illiteracy in her town. She realized that too many people couldn't read. She organized a program where volunteers could be trained to tutor nonreaders. The program was called Literacy Volunteers. It caught on quickly.

The program began in New York State. When the program had existed for about ten years, it spread to other states. Its name changed to Literacy Volunteers of America (LVA).

In 1985, First Lady Barbara Bush became the honorary chair of the LVA National Advisory Council. She has held the position ever since and has helped recruit new volunteers for LVA.

Currently, there are over 100,000 people involved in LVA, both as students and as teachers. There are programs in nearly every state in this country. And LVA is still growing strong.

Libraries often have programs that teach reading.

The Laubach program and LVA are huge, but there are also some small programs that teach reading. Libraries often have programs. Some night schools offer reading help too. There is a fair amount of interest, but it is still not enough to combat the problem. Out of 27 million illiterate adults, only 3 million are helped each year.

HIDING THE PROBLEM

It's not easy to attract people to reading programs. People are usually embarrassed that they can't read. They often hide it from nearly everyone they know. They are afraid of what would happen if people found out.

Ann was scared someone would find out that she couldn't read. She worried about it every day. To fool people, she carried a romance novel in her pocketbook. During her lunch break at the farm market, Ann would pull out the book and pretend to read it. Everybody at work thought she loved to read. She was 45 years old and had been fooling people for a long time.

Ann was lucky. She didn't need to read to do her job. She was friendly and outgoing. She knew a lot about the plants and vegetables that they sold. Even her coworkers came to her for advice.

Her boss was very impressed with Ann's work. She kept trying to promote Ann to manager. She couldn't understand why Ann kept turning her down. But Ann knew that if she became manager, she would have to place the orders. She couldn't read the order forms. If she let herself be promoted, everyone would find out that she couldn't read.

It never occurred to Ann that she could learn to read at age 45. She thought that if she hadn't learned to read in school, then she'd never learn. She didn't know that there were programs that were created just for people like her.

REACHING THE NONREADERS

Reaching these nonreaders is one of the hardest things that literacy programs have to do. In fact, with all the literacy programs in this country, only 4 percent of the nonreaders get help.

Some people think they are too dumb to learn. Others know they are smart, but they have had bad experiences with school and they don't want to go back. Sometimes, the problem is something as simple as not being able to get to a class. Many illiterate people do not have a driver's license.

Literacy programs keep reaching out, though. Some have tried to reach people by putting up signs. As you can imagine, this doesn't work very well. People who can't read aren't in the habit of looking at signs. Even if they did notice the sign, they wouldn't know that it was for them.

LVA advertises on television. They have received many phone calls from people who see their ad. Another way to let people know about reading programs is through churches and other community groups. It's important to get the word out that there *is* help available.

VOLUNTEER TUTORS

It's just as important to reach tutors as it is to reach students. Most of the reading programs teach students one-on-one. That means there has to be one tutor for every student.

A lot of people use excuses to get out of becoming a volunteer. They say they are too busy. But teaching someone to read requires only two hours a week. Other people say they are not good at teaching. But reading programs like LVA show volunteers how to teach.

Some people even say that illiteracy doesn't affect them. They use this as an excuse not to get involved. But the illiteracy problem affects the whole country, not just nonreaders.

The United States ranks 49th in literacy out of all the countries in the United Nations. That means that 48 other countries have a better literacy percentage. That's pretty surprising considering that this country is supposed to be one of the world's leaders.

Illiteracy affects the country in other ways. Three-quarters of the people who are on welfare can't read. If they could read, they might be able to get jobs. Then the country wouldn't have to support them. There are many examples of how national literacy can help everyone.

Teaching someone to read only requires two hours a week.

BUSINESS TROUBLE

Nancy was 62 years old and had worked on the assembly line in the bread factory most of her life. It was boring work, but she couldn't change her job because she couldn't read. She didn't need to read to work on the assembly line.

Then everything changed. The company brought in new machines. These machines were run by computers. They were supposed to make Nancy's job easier. But instead, they made things more difficult.

The company gave Nancy a manual to read. This would teach her how to use the machine. Nancy didn't tell her boss she couldn't read. Instead, she brought the manual home to her husband. He read it to her. Nancy tried to remember everything she heard, but it was tough.

A trainer showed Nancy how to use the machine. She felt a little better. It didn't seem that difficult. But when the trainer left, Nancy had trouble. It wasn't working. She was ruining loaf after loaf of bread because she couldn't get the machine to work properly.

Nancy asked her boss to help her out. He tossed the manual at her. "Just look it up," he said. "And do it quickly. You're costing the company lots of money!"

Nancy burst into tears and ran out the door. She was too embarrassed to tell him she couldn't read.

Some businesses have reading programs for employees who don't read well. The military in this country also offers reading help for the enlisted men and women who have problems. It is worth spending the money to hire teachers because it saves the businesses and the military money in the long run.

The programs in businesses and the military assume that each person already has some reading ability. Otherwise they wouldn't have been hired. There are not many businesses that provide the one-on-one help that beginning readers need.

Businesses lose money when employees can't read. They then have to charge more to make up for their losses. The United Way estimated that illiteracy costs businesses and taxpayers $20 billion every year. Everybody pays when people can't read.

ILLITERACY IN THE PRISONS

Anyone who says that illiteracy isn't a problem in this country should take a look at our prisons. The illiteracy rate is higher among prisoners than among any other group of people. Sixty percent of the people in prisons can't read. And it costs over $7 billion a year to keep these people in prison.

It's even worse in the youth correctional facilities. Almost 85 percent of the people there have reading problems. Most are high school dropouts.

The illiteracy rate is higher among people in prison than among any other group in the United States. Sixty percent of the people in prisons can't read.

It is clear that there is a link between illiteracy and crime. Many of these people probably tried to get jobs and couldn't. No one would hire them because they couldn't read well enough. They had to support themselves somehow, so they turned to crime. Other non-readers feel cheated by society when they can't get jobs. They strike back in anger and end up in jail.

TEACHING

When Roger heard about the literacy problem in the United States, he wanted to help. He went to his local library. They were thrilled to have him volunteer. They needed all the tutors they could get.

The library sent Roger to some literacy classes to make sure that he had good reading skills. It's important that teachers are good readers because nonreaders often blame themselves when they have problems learning to read. Roger's student might put the blame on himself even if the problem was Roger's. It was important that Roger was qualified.

When Roger was through taking his classes, he got his first student. She was a 50-year-old woman named Jeannie. Roger was very nervous until he realized that Jeannie was even more nervous.

They spent the first session getting to know each other. Roger's classes had taught him that it was very important that he and his student feel comfortable with each other. While Roger and Jeannie were talking, they found out that they both loved gardening. Roger decided that a lot of the reading material he would use would be about gardening. That way, they would both be interested in what they were reading.

PHONICS

Roger's classes taught him all about reading. He learned that there are four ways to learn reading skills: *phonics, sight words, pattern words* and *language experience.*

Phonics is putting a sound to each letter. The student memorizes the sound of each letter. Then he or she can

"sound out" words. Many people learn to read this way. In fact, this is what Jeannie was taught in school. But she hated it.

When Roger had Jeannie use phonics, she panicked. She remembered what it had been like in school. She was always embarrassed when she had to read out loud. Her embarrassment made her poor reading skills even worse. The same thing was happening again. Jeannie's mind was blocking the words before she had a chance to sound them out.

Roger knew from his literacy classes to try different methods. What works for one student might not work for another. Phonics was not working for Jeannie. Roger thought it would be better to try a different method.

SIGHT WORDS AND PATTERN WORDS

Roger then tried sight words. Sight words are words that the reader memorizes. These words can't be sounded out. English is funny that way. The word "of" is a good example. If it were spelled the way it sounds, it would be spelled "uv." The word "of" is something that a new reader has to learn as a sight word. Once people become good readers, they have hundreds of sight words. They have learned them without even trying!

Students will learn to read more quickly if they work with material that interests them.

35

Jeannie liked working with sight words. She had a good memory. Roger put the words on flash cards. He would show a word to Jeannie and she would try to remember which word it was. As soon as she learned a word perfectly, Roger would take it out of the stack. He would then add a new word. Before long, Jeannie knew 100 sight words.

Roger decided it was time to combine sight words with pattern words. He thought that pattern words would help Jeannie to get comfortable with phonics. Pattern words are like a combination of phonics and sight words.

For instance, sounding out the word "meat" isn't very easy for the beginning reader. The "e" and the "a" combine to make a sound all of their own. This might have to be a sight word. But once the student learns "meat" as a sight word, he or she doesn't have to learn all the other "eat" words—seat, treat, beat, neat. They all follow the same pattern. All the student has to do is sound out the first letter. Just as Roger thought, Jeannie caught on quickly.

LANGUAGE EXPERIENCE

The fourth method for teaching reading is language experience. This is especially good for adults. Teaching adults to read is a little different from teaching children.

Children are thrilled by very simple books like *The Cat in the Hat*. But most adults become bored with simple books.

This is where language experience comes in. The teacher asks the student to talk about something—a hobby or a trip or a person he or she knows. It can be anything. The teacher writes down everything the student says. Then the student "reads" it back. The teacher helps the student along. The words are familiar because they are the student's own words. The reading is interesting because it is about the student. That is what language experience is all about.

Most adults don't expect learning to read to be fun. They view it as a chore. They expect to read sentences like "Ned has a red bed" or "Sue has a blue hat." Sentences like these are boring. They also don't have a lot of meaning. The purpose of these sentences is to get the student to sound out words. The student doesn't learn to think about what he or she is reading. Language experience makes sure that people do more than learn to read. They also read to learn.

READING FOR FUN

With language experience, it helps if the teacher knows what the student is interested in. For instance, Bob loved planes. He knew them all. It was his dream to learn to be a pilot, but he was already 60 years old and he hadn't learned yet. He couldn't get his pilot's license because he didn't know how to read.

A friend told him it was never too late to learn to read. He told Bob about LVA. Bob joined and soon had his first meeting with his tutor. Her name was Meredith. In the first meeting, Meredith asked Bob why he wanted to learn to read. Bob said his goal was to get his pilot's license. Meredith decided that Bob could learn to read and learn about planes at the same time.

Bob thought that was wonderful. He thought learning to read would be really hard. He remembered how diffi-

It takes about 35 to 40 hours for a person to increase his or her reading ability by one grade level.

cult it had been for him in school. But now he was reading stories and articles about planes. He was always excited about the next class because he wanted to learn more. Because Bob was so eager to read about the planes, he learned to read very quickly.

A NEW SYSTEM

It takes about 35 to 40 hours for a person to increase his or her reading ability by one grade level. But what does this mean? People around the country have different ideas about what is expected in each grade. It is hard to say exactly how well or how poorly a person reads when the grade level measurement is used.

Recently, the federal government gave the Educational Testing Service (ETS) some money to develop a new method for measuring reading ability. Now a person is given a reading level number. The person might be reading at the 200 level or the 325 level. Each level is measured the same way throughout the whole country.

With the old method, anyone who read below the fourth grade reading level was considered illiterate. Using this guideline, the government could say that there are 27 million illiterate Americans.

The ETS scale measures illiteracy differently. Nearly everyone is considered literate to some degree. It is the *level* of literacy that changes.

Think about trying to count the number of tall women in the country, for example. Who decides what is tall and what is not? If 5 feet 6 inches is the average, is everyone who is over that height considered tall? What about someone who is 5 feet 6½ inches? That person is only a little bit taller than average.

But if you have a scale, then people know exactly where they stand in comparison to others. It is no longer a matter of being tall or not tall. People know their height and then they can draw their own conclusions. It is much more helpful to each individual. Of course, it is not helpful for the person who wants to count the number of tall women.

This is a criticism of the ETS scale. It will no longer be easy to count the number of illiterate people in this country. But the ETS scale will help individuals. They will know exactly where they stand compared to everyone else in the country. It will help them figure out where they need to begin working.

With the new system, people find out what their literacy level is by taking three tests. They get a different reading number for each test. The three tests cover the three different types of reading skills that are needed in today's world.

The first test is for *prose literacy*. That is what everyone thinks of when they think of reading. It includes reading newspaper articles, letters, books and poems. In order to be prose literate, people must be able to read and understand these items.

Map reading requires document literacy skills.

The second test covers *document literacy*. This involves being able to fill out forms, figure out indexes and follow maps. It also means being able to read and interpret tables and charts.

The last test is for *quantitative literacy*. This can almost be called "word problems." It includes adding up the numbers on a deposit slip or figuring out the tax deductions on a paycheck.

We can see how these tests work by comparing Barbara and Kathleen. Both of these women took the three tests. The first test was for prose literacy. The first thing they had to do was write about a job they wanted. Both were able to do this, which brought them up to the 200 level.

Another item was a sports article. They had to show that they understood what the article was saying. Both did well at this, which brought them up to 262.

For the third area of the prose literacy test, they had to read a warranty for a washing machine. Barbara had a little trouble with this section, but she got through it. Kathleen, on the other hand, was stumped. She also had trouble with the rest of the test. It was pretty clear that her reading level was around 262. Barbara was able to answer more of the questions. Her prose literacy number was 324.

Then the two women took the document literacy test. For this test, they had to fill out an order form, follow directions on a map and perform many other similar tasks.

Kathleen scored pretty well on this test. She was placed at the 300 level. Barbara scored 260. It was clear that this test focused on different reading skills than the prose literacy test.

On the quantitative test, they were asked to do things like figure out the total number of books needed for three different classes. They were also asked to fill out a catalog order form with three items and find the amount of tax that would be charged. Barbara and Kathleen both scored 270 on the quantitative test.

The three level numbers from the tests aren't added together. They are used separately to figure out where people need help. Different reading problems require developing different literacy skills.

This is the most detailed literacy measurement system we have in this country. It is also one of the few standardized tests that doesn't use multiple choice. Multiple choice makes it possible for a person to guess and get the answer right.

In the new ETS test, the answer is a word, a short sentence or a number. Sometimes it is even an entire business letter. Setting up the test this way protects it against false results.

NOT QUITE PERFECT

This new testing system is very accurate. The whole country can be measured exactly the same way. It makes it easier to know where to begin teaching a non-reader.

Also, it is more practical to use material that a person comes across every day. A person might not care if he or she has achieved the fifth grade reading level, but that person will care if reaching that level makes life easier and more rewarding.

This new testing method is also less insulting than other methods. A 35-year-old man doesn't want to be told that he reads at the second grade level. By using the ETS scale, he can look at his reading progress in a practical way. When he started, he could barely read the name of his street. Now he can read a bus schedule.

There is also a weak side to the new test. The test is measured by achievements in an *adult's* life. It is hard to determine a *child's* reading ability by using this scale. For instance, even if a child is able to read well enough to fill out a checkbook, he or she may have never seen a checkbook before and may not know what to do with it. Therefore, that child would score lower than he or she was supposed to.

It's too early to tell if the ETS scale is going to make a big difference in literacy. But whether it works or not, it

People who have difficulty reading may have a hard time filling out a job application.

is exciting to see something new being done about an old problem.

THE FUTURE

Despite all the studies and numbers, it is still hard to tackle the illiteracy problem. People who have reading difficulties are embarrassed to admit it. They have usually figured out ways to fool people. When illiteracy stays hidden, nobody gets help.

What can be done about this? Programs like LVA and the one in Kentucky help a lot. If they keep growing, more and more people will be reached. There is help out there. More people are being reached every day.

Fortunately, illiteracy isn't getting any worse. It might look like it is because our world is becoming more advanced. Technology requires that people know how to read. With a lot of effort, the literacy rate may someday catch up to technology.

FOR MORE INFORMATION

There is a national literacy hot line people can call if they want to be a student or a teacher. The number is 1-800-228-8813. The hot line has a listing of all the literacy programs in this country and can give people the name and number of someone to call in their area.

People can also contact Literacy Volunteers of America. The address is:

Literacy Volunteers of America
5795 Widewaters Parkway
Syracuse, NY 13214-1846

The phone number is 315-445-8000.

GLOSSARY/INDEX